Jesus AND Muhammad

THE PARALLEL SAYINGS

D0760110

Jesus AND Muhammad

THE PARALLEL SAYINGS

EDITOR

Joey Green

FOREWORD

Dr. Sayyid M. Syeed

INTRODUCTION

Dr. Kenneth Atkinson

Seastone

BERKELEY, CALIFORNIA

The publishers have generously given permission to use quotations from the works
cited on page 187

First Ulysses Press Edition 2003

Published by:
Seastone, an imprint of Ulysses Press
P.O. Box 3440
Berkeley, CA 94703
www.ulyssespress.com

Library of Congress Cataloging-in-Publication Data

Jesus and Muhammad : the parallel sayings / editor, Joey Green; foreword,
Sayyid M. Syeed ; introd., Kenneth Atkinson
          p. cm.
     Includes bibliographical references and index.
     ISBN 1-56975-326-1 (trade : alk. paper)
          1. Islam--Relations--Christianity. 2. Christianity and other religions--Islam.
     3. Hadith--Criticism, interpretation, etc. 4. Muhammad, Prophet, d. 632. 5. Jesus
     Christ--Parables. I. Green, Joey.

BP172 .J45 2002

                                                    297.6'3--dc212002031984

Printed in Canada by Transcontinental Printing

10 9 8 7 6 5 4 3 2 1

Editorial and production: Lynette Ubois, Lily Chou, Claire Chun
Design: Leslie Henriques and Big Fish

Distributed in the United States by Publishers Group West
and in Canada by Raincoast Books

Have we not all one father? Has not one God created us?

MALACHI 2:10

ACKNOWLEDGEMENTS

At Ulysses Press, I am deeply indebted to Ray Riegert, Lynette Ubois, and Lily Chou for their guidance and insights. I am also grateful to Dr. Sayyid M. Syeed for his sage advice, my agent Jeremy Solomon for his wise council, and Claire Chun at Ulysses Press for her meticulousness. Above all, all my love to Debbie, Ashley, and Julia.

—Joey Green

CONTENTS

FOREWORD
by Dr. Sayyid M. Syeed

Muhammad was born approximately 570 years after Jesus. He received his first revelation when he was forty years old.

For Muslims, commonalties between the teachings of Jesus and Muhammad are hardly news. Muhammad did not claim any originality. The religion of Islam that he preached was not a new religion. He carried on the message that Abraham, Moses, and Jesus had taught before him. The Koran makes this clear: "Say, We believe in God, and in what has been revealed to us [Muhammad], and what was revealed to Abraham, Ishmael, Isaac, Jacob, and the Tribes, and in what was given to Moses, Jesus, and the prophets from their Lord. We make no distinction between any of them" (Koran 3:84).

Muslims show equal respect to Moses, Jesus, and Muhammad. In the Koran, God declares: "Verily, We sent down the Torah [to Moses] wherein is guidance and light . . . " (Koran 5:44) and "We gave him [Jesus] the Gospel with its guidance and light . . . " (Koran 5:46).

It is the religious duty of every Muslim to do what Joey Green has done, to go to the sayings of Moses, Jesus, Muhammad, and other religious seers of the past and highlight their common commitment to monotheism and responsible lifestyles connecting humans with their Creator and with one another. The Koran commands Muslims to invite the followers of Moses and Jesus to help them identify common grounds and promote cooperation for doing good and preventing harm. The Koran commands: "Say, O People of the Book [followers of Moses and Jesus]! Come to common terms between you and us, that we will worship none but God, that we will not associate partners with Him, that we erect not from ourselves patrons other than God" (Koran 3:64).

This book provides a wider basis for mutual appreciation and dialogue, showing the common source of inspiration for the family of Abrahamic faiths—Judaism, Christianity, and Islam. The Koran teaches mutual respect for members of the Abrahamic family based on their shared values and heritage. About the followers of Moses, the Koran assures us, "And from the people of Moses, there is a community that leads with truth and establishes justice" (Koran 7:159). At the same time, the Koran emphasizes that, "And nearest among them in affection to the believers will you find those who say 'We are Christians'" (Koran 5:82-83).

After the tragic events of September 11, 2001, we who treasure peace and freedom feel an intense desire to strengthen the bonds between the three Abrahamic faiths. This modest book sends a powerful message of respect for religious pluralism, coupled with the challenge for us all to discover the core values we share in common. The three Abrahamic faiths need to reassess their heritage, determine how they can bring peace and harmony to this society, and build a strong multi-faith model for a world that has now shrunk into a global village. Jewish, Christian, and Muslim religious leaders must step forward and interpret their religious heritage in a way that brings an end to the millennium of distrust and confrontation, and at the same time builds on the common teachings of Abraham, Moses, Jesus, and Muhammad. History has provided us with a unique opportunity to initiate a new millennium of understanding, faith, and harmony.

The United States of America now finds itself with a sizable population of Jews, Christians, and Muslims living together in a pluralist society fully committed to the freedom of religion. Islam, although a relatively new partner on the American scene, shares a similar vision of religious pluralism well suited to this tolerant environment. Together, Christianity and Judaism have succeeded in building a healthy relationship, free from past confrontations and persecution. Islam is ideologically poised to help reinforce this understanding. Committed to a high regard and respect for Moses and Jesus, and tracing its origins to the common Abrahamic heritage, Islam can play a constructive role in widening the scope of Judeo-Christian society to embrace a truly Abrahamic character.

By pioneering a project that brings our attention to the commonalities between the followers of Jesus and Muhammad, Joey Green has stepped forward to help guide not only the Jews, Christians, and Muslims in America toward a common understanding, but the entire human race toward a vision of a harmonious world filled with loving-kindness, mutual respect, and peace.

INTRODUCTION
by Dr. Kenneth Atkinson

Most Christians learn about Islam through distorted images presented in the media.

Although Judaism, Christianity, and Islam all began in the Middle East, only Islam is widely portrayed as a Middle Eastern religion. This shows how little many Westerners actually know about Islam. Most Muslims, like the majority of Jews and Christians, actually live outside the Middle East.

Although many Westerners associate Islam with terrorism, we must not allow a few fanatics to define Islam. Christians would never permit non-Christians to describe Christianity as a violent religion just because Northern Ireland has been plagued by decades of Protestant and Catholic terrorism. Permitting outsiders to define Christianity and Islam only perpetuates mistrust and ignorance, and ultimately fosters a climate that contributes to violence between the practitioners of both faiths. Dialogue between Christians and Muslims is necessary since it breaks down the barriers of ignorance and prejudice that fuel hostility and violence.

The theologian Hans Kung has said that we must first have peace between religions if we are ever to have peace between nations. Because our rapidly emerging global civilization is now, for the first time in history bringing Muslims and Christians into close contact with one another, it is essential that Christians and Muslims learn how to get along.

One way for Christians and Muslims to understand one another is for each to read the scriptural texts of Christianity and Islam, and to study the founders of each religious tradition. We must go back to the sources, namely the classical texts and figures of both religions, if Christians and Muslims are to ever truly understand one another. An examination of Jesus and Muhammad and the scriptures that document their teachings can open a dialogue that recognizes the many similarities between both religions.

"What," you may ask, "do Christians and Muslims have in common with one another?"

Christianity and Islam emerged from the same cultural sphere in the Middle East. Both claim Abraham as their spiritual ancestor. The Christian and Islamic cultural, historical, and religious traditions all emanate from the same geographical and historical source.

Christianity and Islam are religions of ethical monotheism. Both claim that there is only one loving, just God who is the source and sustainer of creation, and who expects humans to love one another.

Christianity and Islam are historical religions. Both believe that God acts through history.

Christianity and Islam are religions of revelation. Christianity and Islam teach that God has communicated or revealed something of God's own self and will in special ways through particular persons for the edification and salvation of humanity.

Both traditions teach that revelation comes through two special vehicles: scriptures and prophets.

Christianity and Islam are both religions of the Book. Followers of both faiths look to their scriptures for guidance.

Prophets are central to both Christianity and Islam. The Christian community considers Jesus part of the ancient Israelite succession of prophets. In the Sermon on the Mount, Jesus discusses the Jewish Scriptures and emphasizes their relevance. He stresses that his teachings do not conflict with earlier Jewish revelation, but are a continuation of the ancient prophetic teachings of the Hebrew Bible. Like Jesus, Muhammad taught that his own ministry was a continuation of what came before. Jesus and Muhammad stressed their connection with previous revelation, which they both considered still valid.

Many Christians will be surprised to learn that Muslims view Christianity in much the same way Christians regard Judaism. Christianity considers itself a continuation of the message spoken by the prophets in the Hebrew Bible. Christianity therefore accepts the Hebrew Bible as a book that still speaks to contemporary Christians. Likewise, Muslims consider the Hebrew Bible and the New Testament to be prophetic revelations that speak to contemporary Muslims.

Moreover, the Koran teaches that although each prophet has his or her own unique characteristics, they all hold one teaching in common, namely their trust in one gracious and merciful God. In the Bible and the Koran, Abraham repudiates idolatry and Jesus preaches righteousness. Islam supports and perpetuates a sense of unity by maintaining that Judaism, Christianity, and Islam are all based on prophetic teachings. Muhammad made it clear that he considered the Hebrew Bible and New Testament sacred scripture when he said: "I believe in whatever Scripture God has sent down" (Koran 42:15). Islam recognizes the validity of other prophetic teachings, since these earlier Jewish and Christian revelations speak of the same God worshiped by Muslims.

For Christians, Jesus—not Muhammad—is the supreme spiritual prophet. The Muslim belief in Muhammad as a prophet, however, does not mean that Christians cannot learn from Muhammad's teachings. The New Testament contains many passages that speak of spiritual openness to others. Like the Hebrew Bible, the New Testament maintains that the God of Abraham is the sovereign God of all peoples. Jesus never opposed the Hebrew Bible laws, nor the Pharisees and Sadducees. Rather, Jesus challenged religious and cultural practices that he believed were insensitive to the true spiritual life. He spoke respectfully of those different from himself as examples of genuine spirituality. Jesus taught a Samaritan woman (John 4:4-42) and showed concern for a Roman soldier (Luke 7:1-10). He even told a parable in which a man of another religious faith—a Samaritan—was the embodiment of true spirituality (Luke 10:30-37).

The New Testament in numerous places describes Jesus' receptiveness to others, a message that is frequently overlooked by many Christians. Islam also speaks openly of other faiths. The

Koran challenges us to a religious competition in goodness. The Koran even extends to Jews and Christians, called the "People of the Book," the following invitation: "O People of the Book! Let us come to common terms between you and us, so that we will worship none but God, that we will not associate partners with Him" (Koran 3:64). The Koran's call for all religions to live a righteous life is an invitation that people of all faith traditions should be willing to accept.

In a Hadith, a tradition about Muhammad, the Prophet says: "The believer is unceasingly in search of wisdom; wherever he finds it, he grabs it." As "People of the Book," Christians and Muslims have much in common, and therefore have much wisdom to teach one another. Christians and Muslims, however, must first return to the sources, the Bible and the Koran, if they are to ever understand one another. Once Christians and Muslims open these books, they will discover that these texts contain the same message, namely that Christians and Muslims are children of the same spiritual ancestor, that Christians and Muslims believe in the same God, and that Christians and Muslims should seek to live in peace together. This wisdom, taught in both the Bible and the Koran, is wisdom that all people should be eager to embrace.

Parallel Sayings,
Different Lives

In the New Testament, Jesus cryptically alludes to someone who will follow him. "I will ask the Father, and He will give you another Counselor to be with you—the Spirit of truth" (John 14:16).

While Christians believe that Jesus was referring to the Holy Spirit, Muslims insist that Jesus was alluding to Muhammad, the prophet of Islam, born in Arabia some 540 years after the death of Jesus. An illiterate yet pious camel-driver, Muhammad frequently retreated to a cave on Mount Hira, just outside his native city of Mecca, to meditate in solitude. Around 610 C.E., the forty-year-old Muhammad, sleeping in the cave, found himself awoken by an overpowering presence. He claimed that the angel Gabriel (the same angel who heralds the birth of Jesus in the New Testament) enveloped him in a tight embrace, forced the breath from his body, and commanded him to "recite" in the name of God. Terrified, the unschooled Muhammad insisted he could not recite anything. Gabriel squeezed tighter and tighter until the word of God spilled from between Muhammad's lips in Arabic.

Muhammad received these divine revelations from the angel Gabriel at many different intervals until his death in 632 C.E. He dictated these eternal verses to his followers, who memorized them

3

d wrote them down on scraps of paper, palm leaves, and animal skins. Within twenty years of Muhammad's death, his followers, assembled the Koran (Arabic for "proclamation" or "recitation"), loosely organizing its 114 *surahs* (or "chapters") from longest to shortest, in no chronological order, but instead creating a timeless stream of divine consciousness. Muslims consider the words of the Koran to be the word of God Himself, not the words of Muhammad, just as Christians consider Jesus to be the word of God made flesh.

Like Jesus before him, Muhammad preached and prophesized God's word, becoming a living embodiment of God's will on how man should live his life. To Muslims, the certainty that Muhammad never learned to read or write, never attended school, never read the Bible, and never had the Bible read to him proves beyond any doubt that the revelations he received which make up the Koran are indeed God's word. Believers also point to the flowing poetry of the Koran, considered the most beautifully written book in the Arabic language, as testimony to its divine origin. (Muslims regard translations of the Koran into other languages to be inadequate interpretations that fail to capture the intricacies, poetic grace, and intimacy of God's revelation in Arabic.)

At first, Muhammad expected Jews and Christians to embrace the Koran as the natural continuation of their ancient heritages. The Koran affirms that God revealed his word to the Jews and the Christians: "Say, We believe in God, and in what has been revealed to us, and what was revealed to Abraham, Ishmael, Isaac, Jacob, and

4

the Tribes, and in what was given to Moses, Jesus, and the prophets from their Lord. We make no distinction between any of them, and to God do we submit" (Koran 3:84). But the Koran declares that these "People of the Book," in writing down these revelations, altered the words and neglected portions of what they were taught, incorporating factual inaccuracies and fabricating other messages into the Bible. God revealed the Koran to Muhammad "to make clear to you much of what you concealed of the Book, and to pass over many things" (Koran 5:15)—in other words, to set the record straight once and for all. While both Judaism and Christianity reject this claim and the Islamic belief that the Koran supersedes the Bible, the different stories presented in the Koran, deemed by Muslims to be the absolute word of God, provide fascinating and inspiring departures from the biblical accounts.

In his revelations, Muhammad reveres Jesus as a prophet, retelling his story with great respect. The Koran tells us that God "made [Jesus,] the son of Mary, and his mother as a sign for mankind" (Koran 23:50), caused Jesus to follow "in the footsteps of the prophets," and "gave him the Gospel with its guidance and light, confirming the Torah [the Five Books of Moses]" (Koran 5:46).

According to the Koran, however, Jesus began his life much differently from the story told in the Gospels. In the New Testament, the angel Gabriel visits the engaged Virgin Mary in Nazareth and tells her that she will, through God, conceive a child who will be the Son of God. The expectant Mary and her husband Joseph travel to Bethlehem to participate in a census. Unable to

5

find a room at the inn, the couple stays in a stable, where the baby Jesus is born. In the Koran, the Virgin Mary, having been supported financially and educated by her uncle Zachariah, moves to the wilderness to continue her studies in solitude. There, the angel Gabriel comes to her and announces that she will give birth to a holy child. More than a year later, the Virgin Mary returns to her family, carrying her newborn baby. When the family accuses her of wrong-doing, the baby Jesus speaks, informing the angry mob that he is a miracle from God and a prophet. The Koran never mentions Joseph, the journey to Bethlehem, the wise men, the star of Bethlehem, or the nativity scene in a manger.

Like the New Testament, the Koran tells us that Jesus preached to Jews, taught a progressive version of Judaism based on reforming religious laws, recruited disciples to help him spread the word of God, and performed miracles. The Koran also attributes miracles to Jesus that are not recorded in the Gospels. The Koran reports that Jesus molded clay into the shape of a bird and then breathed life into it. At the request of his doubting disciples, Jesus makes a table full of food appear. Neither story appears in the New Testament, but both affirm that the Koran holds Jesus in high regard as a messenger of God.

Both the New Testament and the Koran also claim that Jesus was the Messiah, the savior of the Jewish people. However, the Koran flatly rejects the notion that Jesus is the Son of God, calls the concept of the Trinity polytheistic, and denies that Jesus is a god or God Himself. The Koran also contends that Jesus was never crucified, killed, or resurrected. Muslims maintain that God would never endow Jesus with the power to perform miracles and then allow him to be humiliated, tortured, mocked, and killed by his rejoicing enemies. Instead, God rescued Jesus from this fate, raising him to heaven to await his triumphant return at the end of time. God did, however, make Jesus appear to die on the cross, creating the illusion that he had been crucified. (Some Muslims have suggested that the Romans crucified an apparition or a look-alike, possibly even Judas Iscariot.)

Some non-Muslim scholars question how the illiterate Muhammad acquired his knowledge of the Bible and its prophets. They suggest that he crafted many of Islam's doctrines, traditions, and laws from the Jewish and Christian legends he heard told by the Jews of Medina and the Christian communities he visited. Muslims, however, insist that the Koran is the infallible word of God and that the unlettered Muhammad obtained his understanding of the Bible solely through divine revelation. The same can be said of Jesus. While some biblical scholars claim that Jesus acquired his intimate familiarity with the Hebrew Scriptures through extensive study during the many years of his life unreported in the Gospels, many devout Christians believe that Jesus inherently possessed this wealth of information due to his divine nature as the word of God made flesh.

While the theological differences between Christianity and Islam remain vast, the life stories of Jesus and Muhammad teem with distinct parallels.

Both Jesus and Muhammad rose from humble beginnings to proclaim the One God to the world, built upon the revelation of the One God given to the Jews and recorded in the Hebrew Bible. In nearly every case, the ethical lessons Jesus preached—love, compassion, peace, forgiveness, and repentance—match the core values revealed to Muhammad. The two charismatic leaders also proclaimed that the lessons they taught came from God, not themselves. "My teaching is not my own," explained Jesus. "It comes from Him who sent me" (John 7:16). In the Koran, God instructs Muhammad to tell mankind, "I do not say to you, 'I possess the treasures of God.' Nor do I say, 'I know secret things.' Nor do I say to you, 'I am an angel.' I only follow what is revealed to me" (Koran 6:50). Jesus and Muhammad each saw themselves as conduits for God's word.

Both men are said to be descendants of Abraham, the founder of Judaism—the world's first monotheistic religion. In the New Testament, the Gospels of Matthew and Luke go to great lengths to detail the ancestry of Jesus, reporting that his father Joseph was a direct descendant of King David (in accord with the messianic prophecies of Isaiah), who was descended from Abraham and his wife Sarah. Islamic tradition traces Muhammad's lineage back to Ishmael, the son of Abraham and Sarah's maidservant Hagar. In Genesis, God says of Ishmael, "I will make him fruitful and will greatly increase his numbers. He will be the father of twelve rulers, and I will make him into a great nation" (Genesis 17:20). Abraham casts Hagar and Ishmael into the wilderness. According to

8

Islamic tradition, the mother and son settled in Mecca, where Abraham later visited and helped Ishmael build the Kaaba, the sacred cube-shaped shrine that today sits in the center of the Great Mosque and is the focus of the annual Islamic pilgrimage to Mecca.

Both Jesus and Muhammad faced rejection from their own people. When Jesus declared himself the Son of God before the Sanhedrin, the supreme Jewish court ruled that he had blasphemed and, according to the New Testament, turned him over to the Romans. When Muhammad brought the monotheistic Islamic religion to his fellow Arabs in Mecca and pronounced himself God's last and most important Prophet, the avowed polytheists ridiculed him and forced him to flee for his life to Medina. Despite strong opposition, both men stood up against the status quo, preached against social injustice, and struggled to bring people closer to God.

Tradition holds that both leaders ascended to heaven. In the New Testament, Jesus dies on the cross, is resurrected three days later, teaches his disciples for forty days, and then rises to heaven. According to Islamic tradition, Muhammad and the angel Gabriel ascended from the rock atop Mount Moriah in Jerusalem to heaven, where Muhammad spoke to God. He returned from his night journey to spread Islam, the new religion. (Jews believe that on this rock Abraham prepared to sacrifice his son, Isaac, at God's command. Muslims believe that, instead, Abraham prepared his son, Ishmael, for the sacrifice.) Today, the spectacular Dome of the Rock, Islam's third holiest shrine, built on Jerusalem's Temple Mount, encloses that rock.

For all the striking similarities between Jesus and Muhammad, profound differences remain. Jesus never married; Muhammad took several wives. Jesus was a pacifist; Muhammad led Muslim soldiers into battle. The Romans killed Jesus around the age of thirty, in the prime of his life; Muhammad died at the age of sixty-three from natural causes.

The ultimate difference between Jesus and Muhammad is how they are revered by their followers. To Muslims, Muhammad remains a mortal man, not a deity to be worshiped. Unlike Jesus, he does not sit at the right hand of God. He does not mete out justice. He is not a savior who will forgive the sins of mankind. Instead, Muhammad is the Messenger of God, the seal of the prophets. Though divinely inspired, he was a man of this world, buried in a marked grave under the green dome of the Prophet's Mosque in Medina. Jesus, on the other hand, has no earthly resting place. The Church of the Holy Sepulcher in Jerusalem houses the empty tomb from which Jesus is believed to have risen from the dead. Despite these deep differences, both the New Testament and the Koran state that Jesus will return to earth before the Day of Judgment, linking the two religions.

In perhaps the most beautiful parallel between the two men, both Jesus and Muhammad insisted that their spiritually enriching messages were for all humanity. "I have other sheep that are not of this sheep pen," Jesus told his disciples (John 10:16). He would have undoubtedly agreed wholeheartedly with the words recited by Muhammad in the Koran: "All those who believe, and the Jews and the Sabeans and the Christians—any one who believes in God and the Last Day, and does good—will have nothing to fear or regret" (Koran 5:69).

Here then for the first time—placed on the same page for easy comparison—are the sayings and parables of Jesus and the parallel ethical teachings of Muhammad. Christians will be amazed to discover how Muhammad's teachings echo the sayings of Jesus. Muslims will be awed to discover how precisely many of Muhammad's teachings culled from the Koran and Hadith (reliable written testimonies of what Muhammad said and did) match the values expressed by Jesus in the Gospels of the New Testament. I hope this book brings all humanity closer together with the understanding that we all seek a world filled with peace, love, harmony, and mutual tolerance.

The quotes in this book attributed to Jesus are culled from the four Gospels of the New Testament, written in Aramaic and Greek many years after the crucifixion of Jesus. Tradition holds that the Gospels were written by Matthew (one of the apostles), Mark (a disciple from Jerusalem), Luke (a former pagan who accompanied Paul on his missionary travels), and John (another apostle). Church scholars declared the present books of the New Testament as authoritative Scripture by 400 C.E. No writings by Jesus himself are known to exist. Biblical scholars claim that the story of Jesus was transmitted orally for many years and the Gospels were then written, rewritten, and revised by a number of writers. Many scholars question whether any New Testament writers knew Jesus personally. While the Gospels frequently contradict each other and are sometimes inconsistent with historical fact, the New Testament remains the only source of the teachings of Jesus universally accepted by all Christian denominations. Several Christian apocryphal books—most notably the Gospel of Thomas and the Gospel of Philip (both discovered in 1945 by two peasant brothers near Nag Hammadi, Egypt)—contain sayings attributed to Jesus. However, I have selected the quotes from Jesus for this book only from sources recognized as authentic by all mainstream Christian denominations.

The quotes in this book attributed to Muhammad are taken from the Koran and the Hadith ("oral reports"). Muslims believe the Koran to be the word of God as revealed through the angel Gabriel to Muhammad, who recited the divine words to his followers, who collected them into a book, codifying the Koran around 652 C.E., during the reign of Caliph Othman. I have adapted some of the translated quotes from the Koran from archaic English into more contemporary language, consulting several sources to assure accuracy. Regretfully, no translation of the Koran adequately captures the stunning cadence and beauty of the original Arabic.

The Hadith are the words and deeds of Muhammad as recorded by his companions, including the words of God as spoken by Muhammad. The two collections of Hadith considered the most authentic are *Sahih* ("authentic") of Muhammad ibn Isma il al-Bukhari (d. 870 C.E.) and *Sahih* of Abu l-Husayn Muslim ibn al-Hajjaj (d. 875 C.E.). Other collections of Hadith used in this book and considered authentic include those of Ahmad ibn Hanbal (780-855 C.E.), Abu Isa Muhammad al-Tirmidhi (824-892 C.E.), Abu Nu'aym al-Isbahani (d. 1038 C.E.), Iman al-Baihaqi (991-1065 C.E.), Shihab al-Din Yahya al-Suhrawardi (1154-1191 C.E.), and the *Forty Hadith of an-Nawawi* (1233-1277 C.E.).

The Parallel Sayings

Love

Like Jesus before him, Muhammad taught that love for others is the ultimate expression of love for God. Oneness with God, they insisted, compels us to give unconditionally of ourselves through acts of loving-kindness for other human beings. God has boundless love and infinite compassion for humanity, and He especially loves conscious beings who return His love by loving others. Both Jesus and Muhammad preached these ideas and emphasized the virtues of patience, kindness, generosity, respect, and compassion. Both men condemned cruelty, hypocrisy, and arrogance.

"Love one another," commands Jesus in the New Testament (John 13:34). Muhammad echoed this beautiful directive when he declared, "You will see the faithful in their having mercy for one another and in their love for one another and in their kindness towards one another" (Hadith of Bukhari 78:27). Just as Christians strive to emulate the compassionate and forgiving Jesus, Muslims look to the kind and loving Muhammad as a model for their own behavior. Consequently, the followers of both men share the common belief that dedicating yourself to God means sharing God's love for all humanity.

Love your enemies, and pray for those who persecute you, that you may be sons of your Father in heaven.

MATTHEW 5:44,45

Do not hate one another and do not be jealous of one another and do not boycott one another, and be servants of God as brethren.

HADITH OF BUKHARI 78:57

Blessed are the meek, for they will inherit the earth.

MATTHEW 5:5

The servants of the God of Mercy are those who walk upon the earth humbly, and when the ignorant address them, they reply, "Peace!"

KORAN 25:63

Be merciful, just as your Father is merciful.

LUKE 6:36

On those who show compassion, God is the most compassionate.

KORAN 12:64

So in everything, do to others what you would have them do to you, for this sums up the Law and the Prophets.

MATTHEW 7:12

None of you has faith unless he loves for his brother what he loves for himself.

HADITH OF BUKHARI 2:6

He causes the sun to rise on the evil and the good, and sends rain on the righteous and the unrighteous.

MATTHEW 5:45

We have shown man the right way, whether he be thankful or ungrateful.

KORAN 76:3

Which of you fathers, if your son asks for a fish, will give him a snake instead? Or if he asks for an egg, will give him a scorpion? If you then, though you are evil, know how to give good gifts to your children, how much more will your Father in heaven give the Holy Spirit to those who ask him.

LUKE 11:11-13

All [human] creatures are God's children, and those dearest to God are the ones who treat His children kindly.

HADITH OF BAIHAQI

Blessed are the merciful, for they will be shown mercy.

MATTHEW 5:7

Good is the reward for those who do good in this world.

KORAN 39:10

I have other sheep that are not of this sheep pen. I must bring them also. They too will listen to my voice, and there shall be one flock and one shepherd.

JOHN 10:16

All those who believe, and the Jews and the Sabeans and the Christians—anyone who believes in God and the Last Day, and does good—will have nothing to fear or regret.

KORAN 5:69

Haven't you read that at the beginning the Creator "made them male and female" (Genesis 1:27) and said, "For this reason a man will leave his father and mother and be united to his wife, and the two will become one flesh" (Genesis 2:24)? So they are no longer two, but one. Therefore, what God has joined together, let man not separate.

MATTHEW 19:4-6

And one of His signs is that He created spouses for you from among yourselves that you may find comfort with them, and he put love and compassion between you.

KORAN 30:21

Blessed are the poor in spirit, for theirs is the kingdom of heaven.

MATTHEW 5:3

O you who believe! Be patient, and persevere in patience, and be firm, and fear God so you may succeed.

KORAN 3:200

As you enter the home, give it your greeting. If the home is deserving, let your peace rest on it.

MATTHEW 10:12-13

And when you enter houses, salute one another with a good and blessed greeting as from God.

KORAN 24:61

If someone strikes you on the right cheek, turn to him the other also.

MATTHEW 5:39

The strong man is not the good wrestler; the strong man is only he who controls himself when he is angry.

HADITH OF BUKHARI 73:135

Blessed are the peacemakers, for they will be called sons of God.

MATTHEW 5:9

Make peace between your brethren, and fear God, so you will obtain mercy.

KORAN 49:10

God

Both Jesus and Muhammad declared that God is the only true reality, the King of kings, the eternal Father, the Creator of the universe. Both religious leaders proclaimed that nothing is permanent except God. Heaven and earth exist solely because God willed it so, and all existence depends on God, regardless if humans recognize this transcendent reality. God has always existed and always will exist. His grandeur and glory is incomprehensible to mere humans.

Jesus called God his "heavenly Father" and embraced the words spoken by Moses, "Hear O Israel, the Lord our God, the Lord is One" (Mark 12:29-30). Muhammad echoes these monotheistic ideas. Allah, the Arabic name for God, literally means "the one and only God." To Muslims, Allah is the same God worshiped by Jews and Christians. The Koran affirms: "Do not dispute with the followers of the Book [Jews and Christians] . . . . And say, 'We believe in what has been revealed to us [the Koran] and in what has been revealed to you [the Torah and Gospel]. Our God and your God is One, and to Him we surrender'" (Koran 29:46).

I am the Alpha and the Omega, the First and the Last, the
Beginning and the End.

REVELATION 22:13

He is the First and the Last, the Seen and the Hidden, and
He knows all things.

KORAN 57:3

Where two or three come together in my name, there am I
in the midst of them.

MATTHEW 18:20

Don't you see that God knows all that is in the heavens
and earth? Three people do not speak in private, because
He is their fourth; nor do five, because He is their sixth;
nor do fewer or more, because He is with them, wherever
they are.

KORAN 58:7

Heaven and earth will pass away, but my words will never pass away.

MARK 13:31

Everything on the earth will pass away, but the face of your Lord will abide resplendent with majesty and glory.

KORAN 55:26-27

No one can serve two masters. Either he will hate the one and love the other, or he will be devoted to one and despise the other. You cannot serve both God and money.

MATTHEW 6:24

God sets forth a comparison: A man belonging to many partners at odds with each other, and a man devoted entirely to one master. Are the two alike?

KORAN 39:29

I am in the Father and the Father is in me.

JOHN 14:11

We created man; and We know what his soul whispers within him, and We are nearer to him than his jugular vein.

KORAN 50:16

See how the lilies of the field grow. They do not labor or spin. Yet I tell you that not even Solomon in all his splendor was dressed like one of these.

MATTHEW 6:28-29

And it is He who sends down grain from the cloud; and We bring forth by it the buds of all the plants, and from them We bring forth the green foliage, and the close growing rain, and palm trees with sheaths of clustering dates, and gardens of grapes, olives, and pomegranates, alike and unlike. Behold the fruits when they yield and ripen. Truly there are signs in this for people who believe.

KORAN 6:99

All things are possible with God.

MARK 10:27

Do you not know that God has power over all things?

KORAN 2:106

Come to me, all you who are weary and burdened, and I
will give you rest. Take my yoke upon you and learn from
me, for I am gentle and humble in heart, and you will find
rest for your souls. For my yoke is easy and my burden is
light.

MATTHEW 11:28-30

God desires to make your burden light, for man has been
created weak.

KORAN 4:28

He who belongs to God hears what God says. The reason you do not hear is that you do not belong to God.

JOHN 8:47

God does not change what is in people until they change what is in themselves.

KORAN 13:11

Your Father . . . sees what is done in secret. . . . Your Father knows what you need before you ask him.

MATTHEW 6:6, 8

Nothing on earth or in heaven is hidden from God.

KORAN 14:38

The wind blows wherever it pleases. You hear its sound, but you cannot tell where it comes from or where it is going.

JOHN 3:8

No vision perceives Him, but He perceives all vision.

KORAN 6:103

What is the kingdom of God like? What shall I compare it to? It is like a mustard seed, which a man took and planted in his garden. It grew and became a tree, and the birds of the air perched in its branches.

LUKE 13:18

The likeness of those who expend their wealth for the cause of God is that of a grain of corn from which grows seven ears, each ear containing a hundred grains.

KORAN 2:261

Our Father in heaven

hallowed be Your name,

Your kingdom come,

Your will be done on earth as it is in heaven.

Give us today our daily bread.

Forgive us our debts, as we also have forgiven our debtors.

And lead us not into temptation, but deliver us from evil.

MATTHEW 6:9-13

Praise be to God, Lord of the worlds,

The Compassionate, the Merciful,

King of the Day of Judgment.

You alone do we worship, and to You alone do we cry
    for help.

Guide us on the straight path,

The path of those You have blessed, not those with
    whom You are angry, nor who have gone astray.

KORAN 1:1-7

I came into the world to testify to the truth. Everyone on the side of the truth listens to me.

JOHN 18:37

He has created the heavens and the earth to set forth His truth.

KORAN 16:3

Give to Caesar what is Caesar's and to God what is God's.

MARK 12:17

To hear and obey [the authorities] is binding, so long as one is not commanded to disobey [God]. When one is commanded to disobey [God], he shall not hear or obey.

HADITH OF BUKHARI 56:108

God knows your hearts.

LUKE 16:15

God knows your innermost thoughts.

KORAN 3:154

Why do you call me good? No one is good but God
alone.

MARK 10:18

Say, I am only a man like you. It has been revealed to me
that your God is one God. Let whoever hopes to meet his
Lord do good.

KORAN 18:110

My teaching is not my own. It comes from Him who sent me. If anyone chooses to do God's will, he will find out whether my teaching comes from God or whether I speak on my own.

JOHN 7:16-17

I do not say to you, "I possess the treasures of God." Nor do I say, "I know secret things." Nor do I say to you, "I am an angel." I only follow what is revealed to me.

KORAN 6:50

Anyone who has seen me has seen the Father.

JOHN 14:9-10

Whoever sees me [Muhammad] has seen truth.

HADITH OF BUKHARI 87:15

Did I not tell you that if you believed, you would see the glory of God?

JOHN 11:40

Assuredly in the creation of the heavens and earth, and in the alternation of night and day, and in the ships that pass through the sea with what is useful to man, and in the rain that God sends down from heaven, giving life with it to the earth after its death, and by scattering over it all kinds of cattle, and in the change of the winds, and in the clouds that are made to do service between the heaven and earth—are signs for those who understand.

KORAN 2:164

The most important [commandment] is this: "Hear, O Israel, the Lord our God, the Lord is One. Love the Lord your God with all your heart and with all your soul and with all your mind and with all your strength."

MARK 12:29-30

Your God is one God. There is no God but He, the Compassionate, the Merciful.

KORAN 2:163

Wisdom

Muslims believe that God sends prophets and sacred books to teach people their duty to God and humanity. Muhammad, according to Islamic belief, was the last of the prophets. He was preceded by Jesus and the prophets of the Hebrew Bible, including Abraham, Ishmael, Isaac, Jacob, Moses, and David. All these individuals attempted to dispel the darkness of ignorance and enlighten humanity with knowledge of the transcendent reality of the One God.

Muhammad said, "Acquire knowledge. It enables its possessor to distinguish right from wrong. It lights the way to heaven. It is our friend in the desert, our company in solitude, our companion when friendless. It guides us to happiness. It sustains us in misery. It is an ornament among friends, and an armor against enemies" (Hadith).

Like the Koran, the Bible declares that all wisdom stems from a central tenet: There is only one God, a compassionate and merciful God who created the heavens, the earth, and all its inhabitants, and whose omnipotence and glory can be witnessed in His awe-inspiring creation. Both Jesus and Muhammad would agree with the poetic words of the Psalmist: "The heavens declare the glory of God; the skies proclaim the work of His hands. Day after day they pour forth speech; night after night they display knowledge" (Psalm 19:1-2).

All who draw the sword will die by the sword.

MATTHEW 26:52

Whatever misfortune befalls you is a consequence of your deeds.

KORAN 42:30

There is nothing concealed that will not be disclosed, or hidden that will not be made known.

MATTHEW 10:26

God . . . brings forth what is hidden in the heavens and the earth and knows what you hide and what you make manifest.

KORAN 27:25

It is easier for a camel to go through the eye of a needle than for a rich man to enter the kingdom of God.

MARK 10:25

To those who reject Our signs and arrogantly turn away from them, the doors of heaven will not be opened, nor will they enter paradise until the camel passes through the eye of the needle.

KORAN 7:40

Do not give dogs what is sacred; do not throw your pearls to pigs.

MATTHEW 7:6

You truly cannot guide whom you love. But God guides whom He will. And he best knows those who yield to guidance.

KORAN 28:56

The truth will set you free.

JOHN 8:32

O you who believe! You have charge over your own souls.

KORAN 5:105

Let your light shine before men, that they may see your good deeds and praise your Father in heaven.

MATTHEW 5:16

Let him who is present impart knowledge on him who is absent.

HADITH OF BUKHARI 3:37

Watch out! Be on your guard against all kinds of greed; a man's life does not consist in the abundance of his possessions.

LUKE 12:15

The present life is nothing but a pastime and a sport; but truly the next abode is life indeed, if only they knew.

KORAN 29:64

The kingdom of heaven is like a merchant looking for fine pearls. When he found one of great value, he went away and sold everything he had and bought it.

MATTHEW 13:45-46

Whoever is granted wisdom has indeed been given abundant wealth.

KORAN 2:269

Whoever can be trusted with very little can also be trusted with much, and whoever is dishonest with very little will also be dishonest with much.

LUKE 16:10

Whoever performs a good deed shall receive a tenfold reward, but whoever performs an evil deed will be repaid only with a like punishment, and they shall not be treated unjustly.

KORAN 6:160

Therefore everyone who hears these words of mine and puts them into practice is like a wise man who built his house on the rock. The rain came down, the streams rose, and the winds blew and beat against that house; yet it did not fall, because it had its foundation on the rock. But everyone who hears these words of mine and does not put them into practice is like a foolish man who built his house on sand. The rain came down, the streams rose, and the winds blew and beat against that house, and it fell with a great crash.

MATTHEW 7:24-27

Who is better? He who lays the foundation of his building on the fear of God and the desire to please Him, or he who lays the foundation of his building on the edge of an bank eroded by water, which collapses with him into the fire of hell? But God does not guide the wrongdoers. The building they have built will continually cause uneasiness in their hearts, until their hearts are cut in pieces. God is Knowing, Wise.

KORAN 9:109-110

When someone invites you to a wedding feast, do not take the place of honor, for a person more distinguished than you may have been invited. If so, the host who invited both of you will come and say to you, "Give this man your seat." Then, humiliated, you will have to take the least important place. But when you are invited, take the lowest place, so that when your host comes up, he will say to you, "Friend, move up to a better place." Then you will be honored in the presence of all your fellow guests.

LUKE 14:8-10

Whoever fully surrenders his face to God and does good has grasped a sure handle, for unto God is the issue of all things.

KORAN 31:22

Though seeing, they do not see; though hearing, they do not hear or understand.

MATTHEW 13:13

They have hearts with which they do not understand, and they have eyes with which they do not see, and they have ears with which they do not hear.

KORAN 7:179

Stop judging by mere appearances.

JOHN 7:24

Truly, the most worthy of honor in the sight of God is he who is most righteous.

KORAN 49:13

Every kingdom divided against itself will be ruined, and every city or household divided against itself will not stand.

MATTHEW 12:25

Be not like those who became divided amongst themselves and have fallen into disagreement after clear proofs had come to them; a terrible punishment awaits them.

KORAN 3:105

Do not worry about tomorrow, for tomorrow will worry about itself.

MATTHEW 6:34

Surely God knows the hour, and He sends down the rain, and He knows what is in the wombs. But no soul knows what it will earn tomorrow, and no soul knows in what land it will die. Surely God is Knowing, Aware.

KORAN 31:34

What you have said in the dark will be heard in the daylight, and what you have whispered in the ear in the inner rooms will be proclaimed from the roofs.

LUKE 12:3

Truth has come, and falsehood has vanished away. Surely falsehood is a vanishing thing.

KORAN 17:85

Foxes have holes and birds of the air have nests, but the Son of Man has no place to lay his head.

MATTHEW 8:20

Be in the world as if you were a stranger or a traveler.

HADITH OF BUKHARI 76:5

Faith

Through faith, Christianity and Islam tell us, each individual achieves a personal relationship with God, trusting in God's grace and will. Devotion to God helps us persevere in the face of adversity. To Muhammad, faith meant submitting to God's will, abiding by the divine plan of the universe, being at one with the cosmos, achieving inner peace. The closer we get to God and His love, the more content we feel. But faith, Muhammad insisted, requires good works. Likewise, Jesus taught that when we do God's will we bring about the kingdom of heaven on earth, putting ourselves into harmony with the universe. In this way, said Jesus, faith can move mountains.

The Arabic word *Islam* means "submission to the will of God." The Arabic word *Muslim*, conjugated from the word *Islam*, means "one who submits to the will of God." Submitting to God's will means abiding by His moral and ethical laws, doing good deeds, seeking justice, giving to charity, working to make the world a better place. Jesus, too, submitted to God's will in both word and deed. In the Garden of Gethsemane, he prays, "Father, everything is possible for you. Take this cup from me. Yet not what I will, but what you will" (Mark 14:36).

Your eye is the lamp of your body. When your eyes are good, your whole body also is full of light. But when they are bad, your body is also full of darkness. See to it, then, that the light within you is not darkness. Therefore, if your whole body is full of light, and no part of it dark, it will be completely lighted, as when the light of a lamp shines on you.

LUKE 11:34-36

God is the light of the heavens and earth. His light is like a niche in which is a lamp—the lamp encased in glass— the glass, as it were, a glistening star. From a blessed tree it is lighted, the olive, neither of the East nor of the West, whose oil appears to give light even though fire does not touch it. It is light upon light. God guides whoever he pleases to His light, and God sets forth parables for men, for God knows all things.

KORAN 24:35

Your faith has healed you.

MARK 5:34

The Lord of the Worlds—who created me and guides me, who gives me food and drink; And when I am ill, He heals me, and who will cause me to die, and give me life again; And who, I hope, will forgive me my sins on the Day of Judgment.

KORAN 26:77-82

Unless you change and become like little children, you will never enter the kingdom of heaven.

MATTHEW 18:3

Every child is born of the nature of purity and submission to God.

HADITH OF BUKHARI 23:112

The kingdom of God does not come with your careful observation, nor will people say, "Here it is" or "There it is," because the kingdom of God is within you.

LUKE 17:20

Heaven and earth contain me not, but the heart of my faithful servant contains me.

HADITH OF SUHRAWARDI

I have much more to say to you, more than you can now bear. But when he, the Spirit of truth, comes, he will guide you into all truth.

JOHN 16:12-13

If all the trees that are upon the earth were to become pens, and if God should after that swell the seas into seven seas of ink, His words would not be exhausted.

KORAN 31:27

I tell you the truth, if you have faith as small as a mustard seed, you can say to this mountain, "Move from here to there," and it will move. Nothing will be impossible for you.

MATTHEW 17:20

You will see the mountains, which you think are firm, pass away like a flying cloud.

KORAN 27:88

If anyone comes to me and does not hate his father and mother, his wife and children, his brothers and sisters—yes, and even his own life—he cannot be my disciple.

LUKE 14:26

None of you has faith unless I am dearer to him than his father and his son and all mankind.

HADITH OF BUKHARI 2:8

Why does this generation ask for a miraculous sign? I tell you the truth, no sign will be given to it.

MARK 8:12

With their most solemn oath they have sworn by God that if a sign came to them they would certainly believe it. Say, Signs are in the power of God alone; and He does not teach you with signs, because when they were wrought, you did not believe.

KORAN 6:109

Ask and it will be given to you; seek and you will find; knock and the door will be opened to you. For everyone who asks receives; he who seeks finds; and to him who knocks, the door will be opened.

MATTHEW 7:7-8

God has declared: I am close to the thought that My servant has of Me, and I am with him wherever He recollects Me. If he remembers Me in himself, I remember him in Myself, and if he remembers Me in a gathering, I remember him better than those in the gathering do, and if he approaches Me by as much as one hand's length, I approach him by a cubit . . . . If he takes a step towards Me, I run towards him.

HADITH OF IBN HANBAL

Everyone who exalts himself will be humbled, and he who humbles himself will be exalted.

LUKE 18:14

He who has in his heart faith equal to a single grain of mustard seed will not enter hell, and he who has in his heart as much pride as a grain of mustard seed will not enter paradise.

HADITH OF MUSLIM I:165

Peace I leave with you; my peace I give to you. I do not give to you as the world gives.

JOHN 14:27

He it is who sends down peace into the hearts of the faithful that they might add faith to their faith.

KORAN 48:4

Look at the birds of the air; they do not sow or reap or store away in barns, and yet your heavenly Father feeds them.

MATTHEW 6:26

How many animals do not carry their own food! God feeds them and you. He hears, knows all things.

KORAN 29:60

He who is least among you all, he is the greatest.

LUKE 9:48

People are like mines of gold and silver. The more excellent of them in the days of ignorance are the more excellent of them in submission [to God] when they attain knowledge.

HADITH: MISHKAT: MUSLIM 2:1

The secret of the kingdom of God has been given to you. But to those on the outside everything is said in parables so that "they may be ever seeing but never perceiving, and ever hearing but never understanding; otherwise they might turn and be forgiven" (Isaiah 6:9-10).

MARK 4:10-12

He sent down to you the Book. Some of its verses are decisive; these are the essence of the Book, and others are figurative. Those whose hearts err follow the figurative parts, craving discord, craving an interpretation; yet no one knows its interpretation except God. And those firmly rooted in knowledge say, "We believe in it; it is all from our Lord." But no one will bear this in mind, except men of understanding.

KORAN 3:7

When you pray, go into your room, close the door, and pray to your Father, who is unseen.

MATTHEW 6:6

Call on your Lord humbly and in secret.

KORAN 7:55

Take nothing for the journey—no staff, no bag, no bread, no money, no extra tunic.

LUKE 9:3

Provide for the journey, but the best provision is piety.

KORAN 2:197

I am the light of the world. Whoever follows me will never walk in darkness, but will have the light of life.

JOHN 8:12

Those who have shared [the Prophet's] faith, their light will stream before them and on their right hands. They will say, "Lord, perfect our light, and pardon us, for You have power over all things."

KORAN 66:8

This is what the kingdom of God is like. A man scatters seed on the ground. Night and day, whether he sleeps or gets up, the seed sprouts and grows, though he does not know how. All by itself the soil produces grain—first the stalk, then the head, then the full kernel in the head. As soon as the grain is ripe, he puts the sickle to it, because the harvest has come.

MARK 4:26-29

Muhammad is the Apostle of God; and those with him . . . are portrayed in the Gospel like a seed that sends forth its stalk, then strengthens it, so it grows stout and rises on its stem, filling the sower with delight.

KORAN 48:29

And when you pray, do not keep on babbling like the pagans, for they think they will be heard because of their many words.

MATTHEW 6:7

Successful indeed are the believers who are humble in their prayers.

KORAN 23:1-2

Light has come into the world, but men loved darkness instead of light because their deeds were evil. Everyone who does evil hates the light, and will not come into the light for fear that his deeds will be exposed. But whoever lives by the truth comes into the light, so that it may be seen plainly that what he has done has been through God.

JOHN 3:19-21

Indeed a light and a clear Book has come to you from God, by which God will guide him who will follow after His good pleasure, to paths of peace, and will bring them out of the darkness to the light, by His will, and guides them to the straight path.

KORAN 5:15-16

Let the dead bury their own dead, but you go and proclaim the kingdom of God.

LUKE 9:60

You bring forth the living from the dead, and You bring forth the dead from the living.

KORAN 3:27

Law

The Koran, like the Bible, forbids stealing, adultery, lying, and murder. Both Jesus and Muhammad spoke of God's laws, and both men elaborated on the laws God gave to Moses at Mount Sinai. Jesus urged his followers to adhere to the spirit of Jewish law, rather than the letter of the law. He emphasized the ethical aspects of Judaism, guiding his followers toward a deeply spiritual path. Muhammad provided specific directions to his followers on how to conduct themselves in ways that will please God. His words speak of a divine pattern in the universe, elucidating the transcendent will of God as rules of behavior, specifying a comprehensive moral order.

Just as the New Testament heralds Jesus as a new Moses, the Koran elevates Muhammad above both Moses and Jesus, calling him "the seal of the prophets" (Koran 33:40). Like Jesus, he reiterates the laws given to Moses, expounds upon them, and lives his life as an example to be followed. Jesus could have been speaking for Muhammad when he said, "Do not think that I have come to abolish the Law or the Prophets; I have not come to abolish them but to fulfill them" (Matthew 5:17). Similarly, in the Koran, God tells Muhammad, "Nothing has been said to you that has not been said to the apostles before you" (Koran 41:43).

Do not judge, and you will not be judged.

LUKE 6:37

Wrong not, and you will not be wronged.

KORAN 2:279

You know the commandments: "Do not murder, do not commit adultery, do not steal, do not give false testimony, do not defraud, honor your father and mother" (Exodus 20:12-16).

MARK 10:19

Be good to your parents. Do not kill your children because of poverty; We will provide for them and for you. And do not draw near to indecent behavior, in the open or in secret. Do not kill anyone whom God has forbidden, except by way of justice and law. This He has enjoined on you, so you may understand.

And do not draw near the property of the orphan, except to improve it, until he comes of age. Use a full measure and a just balance; We will not task a soul beyond its ability. And when you give judgment, observe justice, even if it concerns a relative, and fulfill God's covenant.

KORAN 6:151-152

With the measure you use, it will be measured to you.

MARK 4:24

Let the recompense of evil be only a like evil, but whoever forgives and is reconciled, shall be rewarded by God Himself.

KORAN 42:40

You have heard that it was said, "Do not commit
adultery" (Exodus 20:14). But I say to you that anyone
who looks at a woman lustfully has already committed
adultery with her in his heart.

MATTHEW 5:27-28

The adultery of the eye is the lustful look, and the
adultery of the tongue is the licentious speech, and the
heart desires and yearns, which the parts may or may not
put into effect.

HADITH OF MUSLIM 33:32

What is highly valued among men is detestable in God's sight.

LUKE 16:15

Do not be extravagant; for God does not love the extravagant.

KORAN 6:141

Why do you look at that speck of sawdust in your brother's eye and pay no attention to the plank in your own eye? How can you say to your brother, "Brother, let me take the speck out of your eye," when you yourself fail to see the plank in your own? You hypocrites, first take the plank out of your eye, and then you will see clearly to remove the speck from your brother's eye.

LUKE 6:41-42

Let not men deride other men who may be better than themselves; nor let women deride other women who may be better than themselves. And do not find fault with one another, nor call one another nicknames . . . . Avoid frequent suspicions, for some suspicions are a sin; and do not spy, nor backbite one another.

KORAN 49:11-12

Simply let your "Yes" be "Yes," and your "No," "No."

MATTHEW 5:37

Do not mix the truth with falsehood, and do not conceal the truth when you know it.

KORAN 2:42

For Moses said: "Honor your father and your mother" (Exodus 20:12), and, "Anyone who curses his father or mother must be put to death" (Exodus 21:17).

MARK 7:10

Be kind to your parents. Whether one or both of them attain old age with you, do not say a contemptuous word to them, nor reproach them, but speak to them both with respectful words. And defer humbly to them out of kindness, and say, "Lord! Have compassion on them both, even as they reared me when I was little."

KORAN 17:23-24

And when you pray, do not be like the hypocrites, for they love to pray standing in the synagogues and on the street corners to be seen by men.

MATTHEW 6:5

And the hypocrites would deceive God, but he will deceive them! When they stand up for prayer, they stand carelessly, to be seen of men, and they remember God but little.

The hypocrites would deceive God, but he will deceive them! When they stand up for prayer, they stand carelessly, to be seen of men, and they remember God but little.

KORAN 4:142

Do not think that I have come to abolish the Law or the Prophets; I have not come to abolish them but to fulfill them. I tell you the truth, until heaven and earth disappear, not the smallest letter, not the least stroke of a pen, will by any means disappear from the Law until everything is accomplished. Anyone who breaks one of the least of these commandments and teaches others to do the same will be called the least in the kingdom of heaven, but whoever practices and teaches these commands will be called great in the kingdom of heaven.

MATTHEW 5:17-19

Surely We have revealed to you [Muhammad] as We revealed to Noah and the prophets after him, as We revealed to Abraham and Ishmael and Isaac and Jacob and the Tribes, and Jesus and Job and Jonah and Aaron and Solomon, and we gave the Psalms to David. And some messengers We have mentioned to you before, and some messengers We have not mentioned to you . . . . Messengers to announce and to warn, that mankind, after those messengers, might have no plea against God. And God is Mighty, Wise.

KORAN 4:163-165

If your hand causes you to sin, cut it off. It is better for you to enter into life maimed than with two hands to go into hell, where the fire never goes out. And if your foot causes you to sin, cut it off. It is better for you to enter life crippled than to have two feet and be thrown into hell. And if your eye causes you to sin, pluck it out. It is better for you to enter the kingdom of God with one eye than to have two eyes and be thrown into hell.

MARK 9:43-47

As for the man who steals and the woman who steals, cut off their hands as punishment for their doings. This is a penalty by way of warning from God Himself. And God is Mighty, Wise. But whoever repents after his wickedness and makes amends, surely God will turn to him; for God is Forgiving, Merciful.

KORAN 5:38-39

Charity

Like Jesus, Muhammad advocated honoring parents, protecting orphans and widows, and giving charity to the needy. Charity, both leaders taught, helps alleviate the suffering of others, bringing about a more just society. In Islam, charity is called *zakat*, an Arabic word that literally means "purity," because giving charity helps us surrender some of our greed, purifying our souls. Paying *zakat* is compulsory, just like the tithe commanded in the Bible. Charitable contributions made beyond the obligatory *zakat* are called *sadaqat* (like the Hebrew word *tzedakah*), meaning "justice" or "righteousness," since giving charity helps correct any injustice in the world.

What we do with money in this life is a true test of our worth as human beings. God bestows wealth upon us as a trust, both leaders taught, to see whether we disperse it to help the needy and oppressed, contributing to the good of all humanity. As Muhammad recited, "Those who are saved from their own greed will prosper" (Koran 59:9). Like Muhammad, Jesus urged people to give up their love of material possessions to focus all their energies on helping others. "If you want to be perfect," Jesus explained, "go, sell your possessions and give to the poor, and you will have treasure in heaven" (Matthew 19:21). Muhammad concurred, "You will never attain righteousness until you give of what you love; and whatever you give, God truly knows it" (Koran 3:92).

Go, sell everything you have and give to the poor, and you will have treasure in heaven. Then come, follow me.

MARK 10:21

He is pious who believes in God and . . . who, for the love of God, gives his wealth to his kindred and to the orphans and the needy and the wayfarer and the beggars and to free the captive.

KORAN 2:177

For I was hungry and you gave me something to eat, I was thirsty and you gave me something to drink, I was a stranger and you invited me in, I needed clothes and you clothed me, I was sick and you looked after me, I was in prison and you came to visit me.

MATTHEW 25:35-36

Whoever alleviates the lot of a needy person, God will alleviate his lot in this world and the next.

FORTY HADITH OF AN-NAWAWI 36

You Pharisees clean the outside of the cup and dish, but inside you are full of greed and wickedness. You foolish people! Did not the one who made the outside make the inside also? But give what is inside the dish to the poor, and everything will be clean for you.

LUKE 11:39-41

As to him who is covetous and bent on riches, and calls
the good a lie, to him will we make easy the path to
misery: And what will his wealth avail him when he goes
down? Truly man's guidance is with Us and Ours, the
Future and the Past. I warn you therefore of the flaming
fire; None will be cast into it but the most wretched—
who has called the truth a lie and turned his back. But the
God-fearing will escape it—who gives away his substance
that he may become pure; And who does not offer favors
to anyone for the sake of recompense, but only as seeking
the face of his Lord the Most High. And surely in the end
he will be well content.

KORAN 92:8-21

A man was going down from Jerusalem to Jericho, when he fell into the hands of robbers. They stripped him of his clothes, beat him, and went away, leaving him half dead. A priest happened to be going down the same road, and when he saw the man, he passed by on the other side. So too, a Levite, when he came to the place and saw him, passed by on the other side. But a Samaritan, as he traveled, came where the man was; and when he saw him, he took pity on him. He went to him and bandaged his wounds, pouring on oil and wine. Then he put the man on his own donkey, took him to an inn and took care of him. The next day, he took out two silver coins and gave them to the innkeeper. "Look after him," he said, "and when I return, I will reimburse you for any extra expense you may have."

Which of these three do you think was a neighbor to the man who fell into hands of the robbers?

LUKE 10:30-37

110

A man traveling along a road felt extremely thirsty and went down a well and drank. When he came up he saw a dog panting with thirst and licking the moist earth. "This animal," the man said, "is suffering from thirst just as much as I was." So he went down the well again, filled his shoe with water, and taking it in his teeth, climbed out of the well and gave the water to the dog. God was pleased with his act and granted him pardon for his sins . . . .

There will be a reward . . . for anyone who gives water to a being that has a tender heart.

HADITH OF BUKHARI 40:11

Freely you have received, freely give.

MATTHEW 10:8

Let not those who are stingy in giving away things that God has granted them from His bounty think that this will be good for them. No, it will be bad for them. For what they hoarded will be hung around their necks on the Day of Resurrection.

KORAN 3:180

When you give a luncheon or a dinner, do not invite your friends, your brothers or relatives, or your rich neighbors; if you do, they may invite you back and so you will be repaid. But when you give a banquet, invite the poor, the crippled, the lame, the blind, and you will be blessed. Although they cannot repay you, you will be repaid at the resurrection of the righteous.

LUKE 14:12-14

Let him who believes in God and the Last Day be generous to his neighbor, and let him who believes in God and the Last Day be generous to his guest.

FORTY HADITH OF AN-NAWAWI 15

Do you see this woman? I came into your house. You did not give me any water for my feet, but she wet my feet with her tears and wiped them with her hair. You did not give me a kiss, but this woman, from the time I entered, has not stopped kissing my feet. You did not put oil on my head, but she has poured perfume on my feet. Therefore, I tell you, her many sins have been forgiven—for she loved much. But he who has been forgiven little loves little.

LUKE 7:44-47

Every good deed is charity, and it is a good deed that you meet your brother with a cheerful countenance and then you pour water from your bucket into the vessel of your brother.

HADITH: MISHKAT:
MUSNAD OF AHMAD IBN HANBAL 6:6

How hard it is for the rich to enter the kingdom of God.

MARK 10:23

Renounce the world and God will love you; renounce what people possess and people will love you.

FORTY HADITH OF AN-NAWAWI 31

When you give to the needy, do not let your left hand know what your right hand is doing, so that your giving may be in secret. Then your Father, who sees what is done in secret, will reward you.

MATTHEW 6:3-4

There is a man who gives a charity and he conceals it so much so that his left hand does not know what his right hand spends.

HADITH OF BUKHARI 24:13

Sin

Both Jesus and Muhammad taught that people have the free will to choose between good and evil. In other words, each of us has the freedom to obey or disobey God's will. We can comply with the moral code of the covenant or transgress it. Both men taught that one sin leads to another, preventing us from realizing our true inner nature and fully embracing our divine spark, distancing us from God. If you err or stray from the path of righteousness, God may forgive you, if you ask for forgiveness with all your heart. Both Jesus and Muhammad taught that God is just and merciful, and wishes for us to repent and atone for our sins so we can enter paradise, returning to God after death.

In the Koran, Muhammad urges believers to supplicate to God: "Know, then, that there is no god but God. Implore Him to forgive your sins and to forgive the believing men and believing women. God knows your activities and your resting places" (Koran 47:19). Both Jesus and Muhammad would undoubtedly concur with the words of the Psalmist who beseeched God to "Hide Your face from my sins, and blot out all my iniquity. Create in me a clean heart, O God, and renew a steadfast spirit within me" (Psalm 51:9-10).

If your brother sins against you, go and show him his fault, just between the two of you. If he listens to you, you have won your brother over.

MATTHEW 18:15

If two parties of believers quarrel, make peace between them. And if one party wrongs the other, oppose the party that did the wrong until they return to the precepts of God. If they return, make peace between them justly, and act equitably. God loves the equitable.

KORAN 49:9

If any one of you is without sin, let him be the first to throw a stone at her.

JOHN 8:7

Happy is the person who finds fault with himself instead of finding fault with others.

HADITH

Watch out for false prophets. They come to you in sheep's clothing, but inwardly they are ferocious wolves.

MATTHEW 7:15

In the last times men will come forth who will fraudulently use religion for worldly ends and wear sheepskins in public to display meekness. Their tongues will be sweeter than sugar, but their hearts will be the hearts of wolves.

HADITH OF TIRMIDHI

Can a blind man lead a blind man? Will they not both fall into a pit?

LUKE 6:39

Who then is more wicked than he who, in his ignorance, invents a lie against God, to mislead men? Surely God does not guide the wicked.

KORAN 6:144

Enter through the narrow gate. For wide is the gate and broad is the road that leads to destruction, and many enter through it. But small is the gate and narrow the road that leads to life, and only a few find it.

MATTHEW 7:13-14

There is no piety in entering your houses at the back, but piety consists in the fear of God. Enter your houses then by their doors; and fear God that it may be well with you.

KORAN 2:189

Whoever blasphemes against the Holy Spirit will never be forgiven; he is guilty of an eternal sin.

MARK 3:29

Woe to every slanderer, defamer.

KORAN 104:1

For if you forgive men when they sin against you, your heavenly Father will also forgive you.

MATTHEW 6:14

If you pardon and overlook and forgive, then surely God is Forgiving, Merciful.

KORAN 64:14

Everyone who sins is a slave to sin.

JOHN 8:34

Surely God does not wrong anyone; they wrong
themselves.

KORAN 10:44

If a man owns a hundred sheep, and one of them wanders away, will he not leave the ninety-nine on the hills and go to look for the one that wandered off? And if he finds it, I tell you the truth, he is happier about that one sheep than about the ninety-nine that did not wander off. In the same way your Father in heaven is not willing that any of these little ones should be lost.

MATTHEW 18:12-14

He who kills anyone, unless it be a person guilty of manslaughter or spreading corruption in the land, will be as though he had killed all humanity; and whoever saves a life will be as though he saved the entire human race.

KORAN 5:32

Call the workers and pay them their wages, beginning with the last ones hired and going on to the first.

MATTHEW 20:8

Every soul will be paid what it has earned, and they will not be wronged.

KORAN 3:25

A man had a fig tree, planted in this vineyard, and he went to look for fruit on it, but did not find any. So he said to the man who took care of the vineyard, "For three years now I've been coming to look for fruit on this fig tree and haven't found any. Cut it down! Why should it use up the soil?"

"Sir," the man replied, "leave it alone for one more year, and I'll dig around it and fertilize it. If it bears fruit next year, fine! If not, then cut it down."

LUKE 13:6-9

Do you not see how God likens a good word to a healthy tree: its roots firmly fixed, and its branches in the sky, yielding its fruit in all seasons by the will of its Lord. God sets forth these parables for men so they may reflect. And an evil word is like an evil tree torn up from the face of the earth, and without strength to stand. God establishes those who believe by His steadfast word both in this life and in the life to come, but He will cause the wicked to err, for God does as He pleases.

KORAN 14:24-27

Stop sinning, or something worse may happen to you.

JOHN 5:14

Let not those who disbelieve imagine that the length of days We give them is good for them. We only give them length of days that they may increase their sins. And they will have a shameful chastisement.

KORAN 3:178

Jihad

Most Westerners and English dictionaries incorrectly define the Arabic word *jihad* as a holy war against infidels. In truth, Muslims are forbidden to use the sword to impose Islam on others. Literally translated, the Arabic word *jihad* means "effort." The word *jihad* more accurately denotes a personal struggle to become a more pious Muslim or to improve the world. The "greater jihad," said Muhammad, is "the struggle against your inner self" (Hadith). A jihad can be an effort to curb hedonistic desires and evil inclinations, conduct missionary work in a hostile environment, study abroad, or give money to charity.

A jihad can also be a physical confrontation against the evils of oppression or injustice—but only in cases of self-defense. Rather than waging war, a true believer avoids violent confrontation, attempting instead to reconcile the situation by conducting a spiritual jihad—using the wisdom of the Koran to persuade wrong-doers to embrace righteousness and truth.

Like Muhammad, Jesus urged his followers to fight oppression and injustice by achieving inner peace and loving others unconditionally, not by embracing violence. Jesus also taught that spiritual advancement requires constant inner struggle. Both leaders would agree with the inspiring words of the prophet Zechariah in the Hebrew Bible: "'Not by might, nor by power, but by my Spirit,' says the Lord Almighty" (Zechariah 4:6).

Blessed are those who are persecuted because of righteousness, for theirs is the kingdom of heaven.

MATTHEW 5:10

The most excellent jihad is the uttering of truth in the presence of an unjust ruler.

HADITH: MISHKAT: TIRMIDHI 17

Do not suppose that I have come to bring peace to the earth. I did not come to bring peace, but a sword. For I have come to turn "a man against his father, and a daughter against her mother, a daughter-in-law against her mother-in-law—a man's enemies will be the members of his own household" (Micah 7:6). Anyone who loves his father or mother more than me is not worthy of me; anyone who loves his son or daughter more than me is not worthy of me.

MATTHEW 10:34-37

O you who believe! Surely, among your wives and your children you have an enemy; therefore beware of them . . . . Your wealth and your children are only a source of trial, but with God is the great reward.

KORAN 64:14-15

No one who puts his hand to the plow and looks back is fit for service in the kingdom of God.

LUKE 9:62

And We will surely test you, until We know the valiant and steadfast among you.

KORAN 47:31

Everyone who has left houses or brothers or sisters
or father or mother or children or fields for my sake
will receive a hundred times as much and will inherit
eternal life.

MATTHEW 19:29

Whoever flees his country for the cause of God will find
in the earth many places of refuge and abundant resources;
and if anyone leaves his home and flies to God and His
Apostle, and then death overtakes him, his reward from
God is sure; for God is Gracious, Merciful.

KORAN 4:100

The teachers of the Law and the Pharisees sit in Moses' seat. So you must obey them and do everything they tell you. But do not do what they do, for they do not practice what they preach.

MATTHEW 23:2-3

O you who believe! Why do you preach what you do not practice? Most hateful is it to God, that you preach what you do not practice.

KORAN 61:2-3

From everyone who has been given much, much will be
demanded.

LUKE 12:48

He has raised some of you above others by various grades,
that He may test you with the gifts He has given you.

KORAN 6:165

The spirit is willing, but the body is weak.

MATTHEW 26:41

Man prays for evil as he prays for good; for man is hasty.

KORAN 17:11

He who is not with me is against me.

LUKE 11:23

But whoever severs himself from the Prophet after that guidance has been manifested to him, and follows any other path than that of the faithful, We will turn our back on him just as he has turned his back on Us, and We will cast him into hell—an evil journey.

KORAN 4:115

Blessed are those who hunger and thirst for righteousness, for they will be filled.

MATTHEW 5:6

Those who believe, and whose hearts rest securely on the thought of God: surely, hearts find repose in the thought of God. For those who believe and work righteousness, blessedness awaits, and a goodly place of return.

KORAN 13:28-29

Blessed are the pure in heart, for they will see God.

MATTHEW 5:8

No soul knows what joy of the eyes are kept hidden for them—as a reward for their good deeds.

KORAN 32:17

Do not work for food that spoils, but for food that endures to eternal life.

JOHN 6:27

The life of this world is made to seem fair to those who disbelieve and scoff at the faithful. But those who fear God will be above them on the Day of Resurrection.

KORAN 2:212

I am sending you out like sheep among wolves. Therefore be as shrewd as snakes and as innocent as doves.

MATTHEW 10:16

God does not burden any soul beyond its capacity.

KORAN 2:286

Be perfect, therefore, as your heavenly Father is perfect.

MATTHEW 5:48

Conform yourselves to the character of God.

HADITH OF ABU NU'AYM

Repent, for the kingdom of heaven is near.

MATTHEW 4:17

⁓

Turn to God with the turning of true penitence; haply your Lord will cancel your evil deeds, and will bring you into the gardens beneath which the rivers flow.

KORAN 66:8

Hereafter

Both Jesus and Muhammad taught that death is the gateway to eternal life. The human soul is eternal, they preached, and continues to exist after our physical death. They declared that God wishes for us to repent and atone for our sins so we can enter paradise after death. Both men insisted that life on earth consists of a series of tests to prepare us for the life to come. Ultimately, we all return to God, who judges the good and the bad. "And the nations will be gathered before Him," Jesus told his followers, "and He will separate the people one from another as a shepherd separates the sheep from the goats" (Matthew 25:32).

Like Jesus, Muhammad believed in the impending Day of Judgment, followed by a journey to either the heavenly gardens of paradise or the fiery pits of hell. "You will not enter paradise as long as you do not have faith," he told his followers, "and you will not have complete faith as long as you do not love one another" (Hadith of Muslim 1:96). These remarkable words eloquently capture the essence of Jesus' teachings.

Do not store up for yourselves treasures on earth, where moth and rust destroy, and where thieves break in and steal. But store up for yourselves treasures in heaven, where moth and rust do not destroy, and where thieves do not break in and steal. For where your treasure is, there your heart will be also.

MATTHEW 6:19-21

Whoever chooses the harvest field of the life to come, We will add to his harvest field. And whoever chooses the harvest field of this life, We will give it to him, but he will have no portion in the life to come.

KORAN 42:20

Whoever has will be given more; whoever does not have,
even what he thinks he has will be taken from him.

LUKE 8:18

Whoever has done an atom's weight of good will see it,
And whoever has done an atom's weight of evil will see it.

KORAN 99:6-8

Those who have done good will rise again to live, and those who have done evil will rise to be condemned.

JOHN 5:29

Whoever does good benefits his own soul; whoever does evil, it is against his own soul: And your Lord will not deal unfairly with His servants.

KORAN 41:46

What good is it for a man to gain the whole world, yet forfeit his soul?

MARK 8:36

Do you prefer the life of this world to the next? But the fruition of this mundane life, compared to that which is to come, is but little.

KORAN 9:38

Do not be afraid of those who kill the body but cannot kill the soul; fear him rather who can destroy both body and soul in hell.

MATTHEW 10:28

Be not like those who forget God, therefore He caused them to forget their own souls.

KORAN 59:19

Men will have to give account on the Day of Judgment for every careless word they have spoken. For by your words you will be acquitted, and by your words you will be condemned.

MATTHEW 12:36-37

Man will have nothing to account for but his efforts, and his efforts will surely be seen: Then he will be recompensed with a most exact recompense, and unto your Lord is the end of all things.

KORAN 53:39-42

The ground of a certain rich man produced a good crop. He thought to himself, "What shall I do? I have no place to store my crops."

Then he said, "This is what I'll do. I will tear down my barns and build bigger ones, and there I will store all my grain and my goods. And I'll say to myself, 'You have plenty of good things laid up for many years. Take life easy; eat, drink, and be merry.'"

But God said to him, "You fool! This very night your life will be demanded from you. Then who will get what you have prepared for yourself?"

This is how it will be with anyone who stores up things for himself but is not rich toward God.

LUKE 12:16-21

The love of pleasures from women and children, and
hoarded treasures of gold and silver, and horses of mark,
and flocks, and cornfields seems beautiful to men. Such is
the enjoyment of this world's life. But the best home is
with God. Say, Shall I tell you of better things than these?
Prepared for those who keep from evil will be gardens
with their Lord, underneath which rivers flow, in which
they will abide, and wives of stainless purity, and
contentment from God.

KORAN 3:14-15

Not everyone who says to me, "Lord, Lord," will enter the kingdom of heaven, but only he who does the will of my Father who is in heaven.

MATTHEW 7:21

Those who have believed and done good deeds, We will bring them into gardens beneath which the rivers flow, where they will abide forever. Therein they will have wives of stainless purity, and We will bring them into a dense shade.

KORAN 4:57

All the nations will be gathered before him, and he will separate the people one from another as a shepherd separates the sheep from the goats. He will put the sheep on his right and the goats on his left.

MATTHEW 25:32-33

Then the people of the right hand—Oh! How happy shall be the people of the right hand! And the people of the left hand—Oh! How wretched shall be the people of the left hand!

KORAN 56:8-9

There was a landowner who planted a vineyard. He put a wall around it, dug a winepress in it, and built a watchtower. Then he rented the vineyard to some farmers and went away on a journey. When the harvest time approached, he sent his servants to the tenants to collect his fruit.

The tenants seized his servants; they beat one, killed another, and stoned a third. Then he sent other servants to them, more than the first time, and the tenants treated them the same way. Last of all, he sent his son to them. "They will respect my son," he said.

But when the tenants saw the son, they said to each other, "This is the heir. Come, let's kill him and take his inheritance." So they took him and threw him out of the vineyard and killed him.

Therefore, when the owner of the vineyard comes, what will he do to those tenants?

MATTHEW 21:33-40

As for the unbelievers, their works are like a mirage in a spacious plane which the thirsty man deems to be water, until, when he comes to it, he discovers it is nothing; and there he discovers God, and he pays him his account in full; and God is swift to take account.

KORAN 24:39

In my Father's house are many rooms.

JOHN 14:2

God has created the seven heavens one over the other.

KORAN 71:15

When a strong man, fully armed, guards his own house, his possessions are safe. But when someone stronger attacks and overpowers him, he takes away the armor in which the man trusted and divides up the spoils.

LUKE 11:21-22

If you can pass through the bounds of the heavens and the earth, then pass through. You cannot pass through them without God's authority.

KORAN 55:33

About the resurrection of the dead—have you not read what God said to you, "I am the God of Abraham, the God of Isaac, and the God of Jacob" (Exodus 3:6)? He is not the God of the dead but of the living.

MATTHEW 22:31-32

Man says: "What! After I am dead, will I really be brought forth alive?" Doesn't he remember that We created him before, when he was nothing?

KORAN 19:66-67

Whatever you bind on earth will be bound in heaven, and whatever you loose on earth will be loosed in heaven.

MATTHEW 18:18

As for that future abode, We assign it to those who do not seek to exalt themselves in the earth or to do any wrong. There is a good end for those who ward off evil. Whoever does good will have a reward better than it, and whoever does evil will not be rewarded for anything except what they did.

KORAN 28:83-84

The kingdom of heaven will be like ten virgins who took their lamps and went out to meet the bridegroom. Five of them were foolish and five of them were wise. The foolish ones took their lamps but did not take any oil with them. . . . The foolish ones said to the wise, "Give us some of your oil; our lamps are going out."

"No," they replied, "there may not be enough for both us and you. Instead, go to those who sell oil and buy some for yourselves." But while they were on their way to buy oil, the bridegroom arrived. The virgins who were ready went in with him to the wedding banquet. And the door was shut.

MATTHEW 25:1-10

One day you will see the believers, men and women, with their light running before them, and on their right hand. Good tidings for you this day of gardens beneath which the rivers flow, in which you will abide forever! This the great bliss!

On that day the hypocrites, both men and women, will say to those who believe, "Tarry for us, so we may kindle our light with yours." It will be said, "Return back, and seek light for yourselves." But between them will be set a wall with a gateway, within which will be the Mercy, and in front, without it, the Torment.

KORAN 57:12-13

There was a rich man who was dressed in purple and fine line and lived in luxury every day. At his gate was laid a beggar named Lazarus, covered with sores and longing to eat what fell from the rich man's table. Even the dogs came and licked his sores.

The time came when the beggar died and the angels carried him to Abraham's side [in heaven]. The rich man also died and was buried. In hell, where he was in torment, he looked up and saw Abraham far away, with Lazarus by his side. So he called to him, "Father Abraham, have pity on me and send Lazarus to dip the tip of his finger in water and cool my tongue, because I am in agony in this fire."

But Abraham replied, "Son, remember that in your lifetime you received your good things, while Lazarus received bad things, but now he is comforted here and you are in agony. And besides all this, between us and you a great chasm has been fixed, so that those who want to go from here to you cannot, nor can anyone cross over from there to us."

LUKE 16:19-26

And the inmates of the fire shall cry to the inmates of paradise, "Pour upon us some water, or of the refreshments God has given you?" They will say, "Truly God has forbidden both to unbelievers, who made their religion a sport and pastime, and whom the life of the world has deceived." This day therefore will We forget them, as they forgot the meeting of this their day, and as they did deny Our signs.

KORAN 7:50-51

The man who loves his life will lose it, while the man who hates his life in this world will keep it for eternal life.

JOHN 12:25

They say: "There is only our life in this world. We die and we live, and nothing destroys us but time." But they have no knowledge of this; it is merely conjecture.

KORAN 45:24

Differences

While Christians can easily accept Muhammad as a great teacher, they cannot embrace him as a prophet who superseded Jesus. Christians can identify with the core values expressed in the Koran, but they reject any suggestion that Jewish and Christian scribes corrupted the words of the Bible or that the Koran transcends the New Testament.

The strict monotheism espoused in the Koran conflicts with Jesus' teaching in the New Testament that the One God consists of three divine Persons: the Father, the Son, and the Holy Spirit. Christian doctrine maintains that God is the Holy Trinity in unity. Muhammad, however, considered Christians who worshiped the Trinity to be idolaters.

While many of the ethical teachings, ideas, and values expressed by Muhammad bear a remarkable resemblance to those preached by Jesus, several contradict Christian doctrine. In the New Testament, Jesus is the only begotten Son of God; the Koran rejects the concept of God having children or being born on earth. Jesus insists that people can only communicate with God through him; Muhammad taught that people must confront God directly. Jesus exalted poverty as a means to greater spirituality; Muslims cannot give away all their money if it deprives their own families of their fixed legal inheritance. Jesus claimed that the Jewish kosher dietary laws are dispensable; the dietary laws of Islam bare a striking similarity to kosher laws.

God so loved the world that he gave his one and only Son, that whoever believes in him shall not perish but have eternal life.

JOHN 3:16

God so loved the world that he gave his one and only Son, that whoever believes in him shall not perish but have eternal life.

Say, He is God alone: God the Eternal. He begets not, and He is not begotten. And there is none like Him.

KORAN II2:I-4

You have heard that it was said to the people long ago,
"Do not break your oath, but keep the oaths you have
made to the Lord" (Numbers 30:3). But I tell you, Do not
swear at all; either by heaven, for it is God's throne; or by
the earth, for it is his footstool.

MATTHEW 5:33-34

God will not punish you for a mistaken word in your
oaths; but he will punish you in regard to an oath taken
seriously.

KORAN 5:89

What goes into a man's mouth does not make him unclean, but what comes out of his mouth, that is what makes him unclean.

MATTHEW 15:11

Oh you who believe! Eat of the good things with which We have supplied you, and give thanks to God if you are His worshipers. He has forbidden you what dies of itself, and blood, and swine's flesh, and that over which any other name than that of God has been invoked. But he who partakes of them by constraint, without lust or willfulness, no sin will be upon him. Surely God is Forgiving, Merciful.

KORAN 2:172-173

You have heard that it was said, "Eye for eye, and tooth for tooth" (Exodus 21:24). But I tell you, Do not resist an evil person.

MATTHEW 5:38-39

We have enacted for them [the Children of Israel] "Life for life, and eye for eye, and nose for nose, and ear for ear, and tooth for tooth, and for wounds retaliation." Whoever compromises it as alms will have therein the expiation of his sins; and whoever will not judge by what God has revealed, such are the transgressors.

KORAN 5:45

This is my blood of the covenant, which is poured out for many for the forgiveness of sins.

MATTHEW 26:28

Say, if you love God, then follow me: God will love you, and forgive your sins, for God is Forgiving, Merciful.

KORAN 3:31

All authority in heaven and on earth has been given to me.

MATTHEW 28:18

Unto God belongs the sovereignty of the heavens and the earth, and all that they contain; and He has power over all things.

KORAN 5:120

I am the resurrection and the life. He who believes in me will live, even though he dies; and whoever lives and believes in me will never die.

JOHN 11:25-26

They did not kill [Jesus], and they did not crucify him, but they had only his likeness. And those who differed about him were in doubt concerning him. They did not have sure knowledge about him, but followed only an opinion, and they did not really kill him, but God took him up to Himself. And God is Mighty, Wise.

KORAN 4:157-158

I am the way and the truth and the life. No one comes to the Father except through me.

JOHN 14:6

God! There is no God but He; the Living, the Eternal. Slumber does not seize Him, nor sleep. To Him belongs all that is in the heavens and the earth. Who is he that can intercede with Him but by His own permission? He knows what came before them and what will come after them. Yet they do not grasp any of His knowledge, except what He wills. His throne reaches over the heavens and the earth, and the upholding of both burdens Him not; and He is the Most High, the Great.

KORAN 2:255

Bibliography

Quotes

CHRISTIAN QUOTES
Holy Bible, New International Version, by International Bible Society (Grand Rapids, Michigan: Zondervan Publishing House, 1984).

ISLAMIC QUOTES
The Koran
    The Koran, translated by J. M. Rodwell (1861). Adapted by Joey Green.

    The Koran, translated by M. H. Shakir (Elmhurst, New York: Tahrike Tarsile Koran, Inc., 2001).

Hadith
    An-Nawawi's Forty Hadith by Ezzeddin Ibrahim and Denys Johnson-Davies (Damascus: Holy Koran Publishing House, 1977).

    A Manual of Hadith by Maulana Muhammad Ali (Columbus, Ohio: Ahmadiyya Anjuman Ishaat Islam Lahore, Inc., 2001).

    Mishkat al-Masabih by Imam Abu Muhammad Husain Baghawi and Imam Waliuddin al-Khatib-ul-Umri, translated by James Robson (Lahore, Pakistan: Sh. Muhammad Ashraf, 1970).

    Muhammad and the Islamic Tradition by Emile Dermenghem, translated from French by J. M. Watt (Woodstock, New York: Overlook Press, 1981).

    Sahih Muslim, Volume 1, translated by Abdul Hamid Siddiqi (New Delhi: Khitab Bhavan, 1977).

Sayings of Muhammad, translated by Ghazi Ahmad (Lahore, Pakistan: Sh. Muhammad Ashraf, 1968).

Science in Medieval Islam by Howard R. Turner (Austin: University of Texas Press, 1995).

Traditions of the Prophet, compiled by Javad Nurbakhsh (New York: Khaniqahi-Nimatullahi Publications, 1981).

The Translation of the Meanings of Sahih al-Bukhari, Revised Edition, Volume 8, by Muhammad Muhsin Khan (New Delhi: Khitab Bhavan, 1987).

World Scripture: A Comparative Anthology of Sacred Texts, edited by Andrew Wilson (St. Paul, Minnesota: Paragon House, 1995).

Reference

Biblical Literacy by Rabbi Joseph Telushkin (New York: William Morrow, 1997).

The Book of Jewish Knowledge by Nathan Ausubel (New York: Crown, 1964).

The Concise Encyclopedia of Islam by Cyril Glassé (New York: HarperCollins, 1989).

The Gospel According to Jesus by Stephen Mitchell (New York: HarperCollins, 1991).

"In the Beginning, There Were the Holy Books" by Kenneth L. Woodward, *Newsweek*, February 11, 2002, pp. 51-57.

Jesus in the Qur'an by Geoffrey Parrinder (New York: Barnes & Noble, 1965).

Muhammad: A Biography of the Prophet by Karen Armstrong (San Francisco: HarperSanFrancisco, 1992).

The Religion of Islam by Maulana Muhammad Ali (Columbus, Ohio: Ahmadiyya Anjuman Isha'at Islam, 1990).

World Religions: From Ancient History to the Present, edited by Geofrey Parrinder (New York: Facts on File, 1985).

World Scripture: A Comparative Anthology of Sacred Texts, edited by Andrew Wilson (St. Paul, Minnesota: Paragon House, 1995).

Index of Quotes

The Bible

Koran

Hadith

Copyright page continued

JOEY GREEN, the author of more than twenty books, including *Jesus and Moses: The Parallel Sayings*, *The Zen of Oz*, and *The Road to Success Is Paved with Failure*, has appeared on *The Tonight Show with Jay Leno*, *The Rosie O'Donnell Show*, *Today*, *The View*, *The Conan O'Brien Show*, *Dateline NBC*, and *Good Morning America*. He has been profiled in the *New York Times*, *People*, *Entertainment Weekly*, and *The Los Angeles Times*. A former contributing editor to *National Lampoon* and a former advertising copywriter at J. Walter Thompson, Green is a graduate of Cornell University, practices Judaism, and backpacked around the world for two years on his honeymoon.

DR. SAYYID M. SYEED is Secretary General of the Islamic Society of North America, a national umbrella organization with more than 300 affiliates across the U.S. and Canada. He holds a Ph.D. in Sociolinguistics from Indiana University at Bloomington, served as Director of Academic Outreach at the International Institute of Islamic Thought, and was editor-in-chief of the *American Journal of Islamic Social Sciences*. He has appeared on the *McNeill-Lehrer Report*, *Today*, and *CNN Crossfire*.

DR. KENNETH ATKINSON holds a Ph.D. in Biblical Literature from Temple University and a Masters of Divinity degree from the University of Chicago. An Assistant Professor of Religion at the University of Northern Iowa, he is the author of *An Intertextual Study of the Psalms of Solomon*. His scholarly writings on biblical literature and the Dead Sea Scrolls have appeared in numerous academic journals.